RECLAIMING MY EDGES

RECLAIMING MY EDGES

KACEE KEMIAH

ShaBazz Enterprise Publishing

Contents

Poems by Topics — ix
Forward by Robin Campbell, PhD — xi
Dedication — xv

1. RECLAIMING MY EDGES — 1
2. OUT LOUD — 4
3. TIP TOP — 6
4. CAN YOU DO ARITHMETIC, NIGGA CAN YOU ADD? — 8
5. I AM QUEEN HEAR ME ROAR — 11
6. DIVA FOR LIFE — 13
7. KEEPING IT REAL — 15
8. I'M ON SOME VIBRANIUM TYPE OF ISH — 17
9. SHE COLD WIT IT! — 20
10. FULL STEAM AHEAD — 22
11. DIVINE PROTECTION — 24
12. THE BEST TICKET IN TOWN — 26
13. CHECK ME, IF YOU CAN — 29
14. NASTY NICE — 33

15	FULL OF SHIT AND TEARS	36
16	SOLD A DREAM	38
17	PROFILE	41
18	AFTER THE CLUB AND LONELY	43
19	HE CAME ON SO STRONG	44
20	IT'S BEEN REAL	47
21	F__K BOY	49
22	DISILLUSIONED	51
23	I CAN'T MAKE MYSELF CRY	54
24	DON'T LET THE SMOOTH TASTE FOOL YOU	55
25	PAINFULLY DROWNING	58
26	IS IT REAL OR MEMOREX	60
27	THIS AIN'T YOUR HEART	61
28	WHEN THE HOT BURNING LOVES TURNS LUKEWARM	63
29	YOU LOVING ME IS EASY?	65
30	INEVITABLE	67
31	HYPNOTIZED BY LIES	69
32	LOST	71
33	OLD NEW SHIT	73
34	4 of CLUBS	75
35	I STILL WANT A KING	77
36	HIM AND ME 4 LIFE AND THEN SOME	79
37	It IS AMAZING To ME ENGLISH AND SPANISH	81

38	ALL I WANTED TO DO IS SKIP TO THE LOU WITH MY BOO	83
39	NOT SURE ABOUT WHAT MAY HAPPEN	85
40	GOOD BROTHERS	87
41	NEGRO PLEASE NEVER EVER GET RIPPED OPEN	90
42	MAD	92
43	BLACK QUEEN IN THE EYE OF THE STORM	95
44	JUNETEENTH	97
45	POMONA, CA	100
46	WORD PLAY	106
47	HOT FLASH	108
48	LACTOSE INTOLERANT	110
49	WHY WOULD YOU WEAR YOUR PAJAMAS TO THE DMV?	112
50	HEAVENLY BOUND BUT NO EARTHLY GOOD	114
51	THE RETURN OF THE SPARKLE	117
52	MEMORY LANE	119

About The Author   121

Poems by Topics

Empowerment Poems   Page 1

Men Shit Poems   Page 39

Positive Men Poems   Page 80

Social Injustice Poems Page 92

Fun Poems   Page 101

Forward by Robin Campbell, PhD

I first met Kim Braxton 20 years ago at the state hospital. I "met" Kacee Kemiah much later. We were both relatively new clinicians at the state hospital. We spent many hours together, eating lunch in the social work office (hers was much more comfortable than mine) or walking around the hospital grounds. At first, we talked about our patients and work and finally, more carefully, about ourselves. We began to spend time together outside of work – we met each other's children, and spent time just having fun. From the beginning, I liked Kim because she was smart, a little off-beat, kind, and funny. Hilarious, really. Sharp, witty, and wry. I learned that she accepts people as they are, but she is not naïve. She is empathetic and takes-no-bullshit. She has a love for language and words and savors a well-turned phrase. This was my first hint that she was a poet. Kim has a way of paying attention to people that is almost palpable. The first time she turned the full weight of that attention on me, I was telling her some trivial story. I remember flinching back a little and I wanted to look over my shoulder to see if there was someone behind me. People don't usually listen like that – as if what you say matters. When someone listens to you like that, it changes you. It makes you see yourself a little differently, because you must be a person worth listening to.

What do I love about Kim? Well, she has a great laugh. Her laugh makes me laugh. Of course, she has all the qualities you would expect in a friend – she is trustworthy, supportive, and open hearted. However, I have come to treasure the unexpected from her. When she tells you a story, I guarantee that it will end somewhere you never would have predicted. She has an appreciation for charm school and Toastmasters (yes – the public speaking group. I know!). Kim does not like speaking in public. Not at all – avoids it like the plague. She made herself go to Toastmasters to overcome her fear, which is pretty genius. It was something I never would have thought of. As she wrote her poetry, she realized that she needed to share it with others, which was a very, very big obstacle. So – she created Kacee Kemiah to be her voice. The solution was elegant and unexpected, which I love. This is Kim Braxton in a nutshell. Do what you need to do, to do what you need to do.

Kim has an unselfconscious delight in the world around her. Art, history, culture, nature – she drinks it all in without hesitation – it is these experiences that provide the raw material for her poetry. Oh! And of course, the people. No matter where or when, folks talk to her. Kim shakes her head in all the right places, laughs at the right times, and sees into the heart of the matter. She hears them. I have seen her talk to hundreds of people, from her patients, ladies on a bus in China, strangers on the metro a world away. When people talk to her, they sit a little straighter, their gaze becomes more direct, their voices are clearer and stronger. Because she listens so intently.

Like many people, Kim has been an outsider, observing others at a distance. That is why she has stories to tell. As a child, there were times when she joined in with the other kids and times when she watched them, aware of the distance between them. While other students were enjoying the freedom of college life, she was juggling work and school and family. Kim has insider knowledge and an outsider's perspective. She weaves together shared experience and feelings of being separate. That is why her work is so powerful.

So, who is Kim Braxton and why should you read her book? First, because she is one of the most honest people I know. She pulls no punches, she does not mince her words, and she speaks her mind. But (and it is a big but), there are parts of her that she keeps hidden and well protected. If you don't ask, she may not tell you what she thinks. She does not give her trust easily, but when she does, it is precious. This book is a gift of trust. When you read it, I hope that you recognize yourself in the sound of her voice as Kacee speaks. And I hope that your voice will be stronger because of it. Maybe you lost your voice because no one was listening. Maybe your voice has become so small that it can't be heard over the clamor of the world. I want you to know that there are people who listen. You are about to meet one of them.

Robin Campbell, Ph.D.

Copyright © 2022 by Kacee Kemiah

All rights reserved. No part of this book may be reproduced in any manner whatsoever without written permission except in the case of brief quotations embodied in critical articles and reviews.

First Printing, 2022

Acknowledgements

The writing of this book has been an incredible journey. First and foremost I give honor to God for giving me the strength and courage to embark on this creative journey. I pay homage to the Ancestors for allowing me to openly share my memoirs. I am extremely grateful to my mother, Marla Stewart, who has supported me in every way imaginable. I thank my sister, Yulonda Smith for being my sounding board and best friend. I express gratitiude to my family and friends and a shout out to my children, La'Vion Ferrell and Ka'Juan Ferrell, for encouraging me and believing in me. I am grateful to my dearly departed daughter, Charity White Shabazz. I thank Melissa Cueva for dragging me to Open Mic, Dr. Robin Campbell for being a great friend and for the writing my Forward for this book, RUPO Riverside Underground Performance Organization and all the artists at RUPO who supported and encouraged me. Thank you to Mario Sandoval for being a great MC and for providing a space, to my sister Robin Richards for putting a smile on my face. Additionally, I would like to thank my publisher, Dr. Sarah ShaBazz and Aminah for the cover art. Last but never the least, Noe Gonzalez, for helping me to find the name Kacee Kemiah, (Great Queen). Thank you to anyone I have forgotten who was instrumental in this project.

I

RECLAIMING MY EDGES

My black hair, my beautiful black coily hair
Why? Why? So much about my hair do I care?
Why in beauty? Do you think I don't share?
Every morning in the mirror I stare
Full aware before I boldly declare:

I am reclaiming my edges

Age 7, I cut off every ponytail that I had
I knew immediately I had done something bad
A mortal enemy of my tresses I had made
Barbershop was a game I shouldn't have played

The love affair with my hair was over quick
Suddenly I was a bald-head chick
In the pit of my stomach I felt sick
For many years, I would have wounds to lick

My punishment was fast, it was super swift
I created this rift and killed the gift

My beauty was now in the eye of the beholder
Suddenly my world was colder

Hours and hours in the beauty parlor getting my hair done
I should have been out having fun
Tortured the whole god dam day
Trying to look a certain way

Tightly pulled braids i could feel my head explode
Dreams of my beauty sold
Fell victim to what i was told

I had way too many perms and ass long weaves
Hair pressure to relieve
New hairstyles to conceive
Failed attempts to deceive
White standard of beauty I tried to achieve

I'm reclaiming me and my lost edges

My hair is no longer a thorn in hedges
Each strand to you I make to new pledges
No more chemicals and fuck that slick look
Cause it's my strength, my growth and my edges it took
Time for a new story in my look book
Your standard of beauty that myth has been shook

All that perm did to my hair was fry it…
It's not my truth so……. I didn't have to buy it
I now accept who I am and boldly defy it
my afro strong and I'm super excited
I know when I enter a room that I light it

I'm reclaiming my edges daily as they grow back
I decided it's time to give it some slack
No longer my hair will I attack
And no more love will it ever lack

So, I apologize wholeheartedly to my crown
This glorious hair on my head
Apply some grease and off to bed
Rock some twisty locks instead

My standard of beauty is redefined
As I look in the mirror, the standard is mine

I have reclaimed my edges
I have reclaimed my pride
My nappy hair I will no longer hide
The natural hair gods they on my side
It's my hair journey and I'm along for the ride

I have reclaimed my edges
And they will suffer no more
I'll get what need from my own beauty supply store
But I might, I said I might
Just rock a good wig every now and again.

2

OUT LOUD

I plan to live my life **OUT LOUD**
Front in center in front of a crowd
Talking about shit that **feeds** my soul
It makes me feel **COMPLETE** …. It makes me feel whole
Writer, poet, Spoken word artist? Is that my goal?
Dreams of spitting **LOUDLY** at the Hollywood Bowl

Speaking about stuff, I've been scared to say
I'm not holding back, no more, not today
If you're a hindrance best get the fuck out my way
Those Bullshit games, I won't continue to play!

No more holding back my thoughts or my words,
Afraid to share my **GEMS** that was totally absurd
I finally **CHOOSE** and **WANT** my voice to be heard
CHIRP, CHIRP, CHIRP……I'M A BLACK BIRD

Loud, clear, vocal and full of passion
No more writing, hiding and stashing
It might be you to get this Tongue lashing

But I'll   give it to you in the latest fashion.

I want to live my life like its Golden
No one on **THIS EARTH** to that I am beholden
I'm playing my hand,   no longer am I folding
Long gone are the days of olden

I want to live my life **out loud** and to the fullest
I remember in high school when they voted me the coolest!
They were right then and they still right now
I can accept that compliment and take my bow.

I have always tried super hard to please
Sugarcoat it and make it go down with ease
Make you believe you was the bees knees
Time to unlock my life **where are my keys?**

I want to live my life **WHOLE** and be complete
Singing and dancing all in the streets
I want to live my life and be very strong
I need enough time to right my wrongs
I want to live my life In **AWE until I die**
No questions asked or me wondering why
LOVE ALL whom I LOVE….. then say goodbye
Close my eyes Take my last breath and let out my final sigh!
But meanwhile, until then… I'M LIVIN MY LIFE OUTLOUD

3

TIP TOP

To the tip, to the tip, to the tip, to the top
You ain't got enough juice to make me stop
Livin' Lovin or listenin' to Hop Hop
Drinking champagne and making bottles pop

Following my dreams trying to figure shit out
I'm on a quest find out what it's all about
Secure and confident .....no more doubt
Stay in your lane......... I know my route

To the tip, to the tip, to the top, I rise
No more hiding and no more disguise
Always learning cause I got three eyes
No fools invited only the wise

To the tip, to the tip, to the top, I soar
A much better person than I was before
Cool with what I got but I always get more
They closed one door and opened four more

To the tip, to the tip to the top, I go
You like my poems? You like my flow?
Smile or something to let me know
Sometimes a sister like me get low

To the tip, to the tip to the tip to the end
I like it here because I made new friends.

4

CAN YOU DO ARITHMETIC, NIGGA CAN YOU ADD?

Subtract my insecurities, my toxic tongue,
and my forever ability to be on guard
Breaking down my wall may be hard
But it's the best Rubik cube that you will ever twist

Multiply that by my intellect and you will find that
I exponentially far exceed any quadratic formula
That you ever tried to solve
Melt my walls with 3 pounds of sugar, I'll dissolve

Deep into 200 pounds of his sweet chocolateness
One day without this kiss …. You will miss
You know what I'm talkin' bout SIS

He may have 99 problems but I ain't one
I like to lay up, kick back and enjoy the sun

I'm talking Two tons of big fun
After this cookie, he won't walk nor run
After round two he's knocked out..... he's DONE

SLEEP?.......Wake up nigga and pull my trigger

Divide my love and conquer my fear
I'm wise beyond 100 years
Smarter than Goldilocks and all 3 bears

Let this gray hair fool you if you must
You know how many crap games I bust?
NO snake eyes for me, I rolls 7 and 11
Ain't no place better than Kacee heaven

Add me to your life, I'll increase your wealth
You're not getting my money, I'm talking good mental health
I'll nurse you back to well, if you get sick
That's how I do my Arithmetic
NEGRO can you add?

Good TIMES, Good SEX and good CONVERSATION
Spend time together no hesitation
I'll have your ass on the phone making a reservation
Be sure that Trust and love is our final destination

The sum of all total is the bottom line
I drink beer, champagne and wine
AND SOME HARD ON OCCASION
69 days out the year!
Put it all together and I'm a good bet
Me and you together on that jet
Ain't you glad me and you met?
Come on baby, Let's Get wet

THEN
Make laugh cause I love how you amuse me
Play your role and never abuse thee
CAUSE
I'm a cold piece from way back
I'll Keep the King and throw back the Jack
Bad and Bougie and a little bit of floozy
You got the nine I got the UZI

I'm a down ass chick, that's why they call me bad
I'm the Sweetest piece that you ever had.
My final question to you is
negro can you add?

5

I AM QUEEN HEAR ME ROAR

"I am queen hear me roar
Better yet, watch me soar"

A young princess knows that it takes time to become a Queen
I have a minute to explain what I mean
It takes time to become a full fledge queen
Build your power behind the scene
More to life than to just cook or clean

Develop your intellect and your skills
Learn how to prepare meals and pay bills
Walk gracefully in high heels
All while closing important deals

Never afraid to claim being a queen
Accept nothing less or in between
Stand up straight, strong and proud

Never afraid to say it loud

"I am queen hear me roar
Better yet, watch me soar"

Full of wisdom, strength, soul and grace
Cheek bone structure of a queen's face
Deep set eyes and a bold nose
Manicured hands and polished toes

Luscious full sized lips
Voluptuous curvy hips
All that and a bag a chips
Full command of a thousand ships

That crown fits because it's custom made
Hard working and fully paid
Strong legacy that will never fade
I receive all accolades

I am queen and I'm ready to rule:
"bring my crown and my septor
My sash and the royal jewels
Prepare my throne as it's time to cut the scrolls
And send out the final decree over all the land"

"I am queen hear me roar
Better yet, watch me soar"

6

DIVA FOR LIFE

A DIVA is a sister who has her mind right and hair tight
Productive in the day and party at night, no curfew in sight

The men all pause as she enters the room
Trying to get close to smell her perfume
Dressed to impress and sexy as hell
Stand up FELLAS and ring a that bell

As she takes her seat and orders a drink
She sees it in your eyes man...What you think?
That a DIVA is a lady with style and class
And in a good mood she'll rock you a pass
Don't piss her off or she'll cut that ass
You ever see a chick so fly that need her own glass
Don't get it twisted, a diva don't just look like this walk like that and talk big shit
She about her business, smart, clever, she on hit
Straight legit and won't NEVER quit
You won't ever catch a diva not on her shit
She's a DIVA for many reasons

Winter, Spring, Summer, Fall. YES...ALL seasons
In the Mix, working and having fun
A DIVA for Life and then some

7

KEEPING IT REAL

Can we for just for a minute keep It real
We all want to live a life ideal
Live life fully and truly feel
express our feelings and keep it real

But life will throw you one helluva curve ball
Run real fast watch you trip and fall
Sometimes into a cement brick wall
Pick up the phone and there is no one to call

So, you get back up and try it again
You don't accept defeat, you still try to win
live a good life but there's too much sin
Look in the mirror and try to begin

To understand that it's hard out here, every day is rough
Solve one problem and another comes quick enough
You need thick skin you have to be tough
You can't just walk around and huff and puff

it will blow your house down
Burned beyond repair
But I refuse to live in fear
Time to clean it up and clear the air

And to this problem there is no easy fix
No matter how you shuffle and remix
You feel beat down with stones and stix
And the devil served you up with his best trick

I understand how exactly how this shit feel
It's getting harder and harder for me to keep it real
My heart needs some relief and some time to heal
I'm ready to give up and cut a new deal

This realness it too much for me to bare
But no one said that life would be fair

8

I'M ON SOME VIBRANIUM TYPE OF ISH

Got me WA KAN DEER-ING ABOUT EVERYTHING

Words designed to bypass eyes and delve deep into your soul
With a gut-wrenching piercing effect
Sharp enough to prick but smooth enough to soothe

Penetrating your epidermis with witty, raw, uncut poetic justice
THAT will make you ASK yourself, "Is she talking TO ME"
OR "IS SHE TALKING ABOUT ME"

Have you WA-KAN DEERING--ING about some ISH
You think you forgot about
A Reminder of how strong you HAD to be
to pull through that Bull Crap mess you got through

Have you searching for the Purple Heart Light
LOOKING HIGH AND LOOKING LOW
PRAYING YOU find some VIBRANIUM TYPE OF ISH for yourself

Make you step your game up.. so you don't get gamed on
Have you slam dunking from half-court, Every game a Triple Double

Powered by a force that will jet rocket you
to new heights and new horizons
you never imagined existed
KIND of like my first visit to a foreign country
and a whole new experience
Busting my third eye wide open

Thought provoking words that become so crystal clear
that you think you are hearing them for the first time
you know like when Pastor steps on your toes in church
and you slowly have to slide them back underneath the pew
in the realization that he is talking about you.
(DO THIS IN AFRICAN VOIVE)
VIBRANIUM TYPE of SHIT that will make you
WA-KAN DOO old goals,
AND dreams that you once had
Dig them up, dust them off and chase them down
With the speed and grace of the Panther

Criss-Crossed bracelets capable of warding off the
Negativity of Dream Killers and Joy Crushers
Rendering you immune because you've become Impenetrable

Super Natural….Intuitive power that exposes friends from foes
A force of illuminating light that will either make them
Disappear, shine brighter or just fucking melt

I now possess that Soul surviving, WA-KAN DOO mystical power
"I'm rubber and you're glue, whatever bounces off me sticks to You"
"Sticks and Stones my break my bones but your names will

never hurt me"
THAT TYPE OF VIBRANIUM ISH

No more procrastination, excuse making, side-tracked, LAZY
complacent in mediocracy or just plain afraid
"I say No more"

I'm on some NOW OR NEVER, TIME TO MAKE IT HAPPEN
LET'S GET IT DONE, WHAT'S THE DEAL and THE HOLD UP?
BECAUSE......I'M ready
Determined, Unstoppable, Unwavering and Unapologetic,
I'm on that type of VIBRANIUM ISH

My reactivated, re-stitched old bags have been
Re-weaved into new designer luggage, strong and durable
Made for traveling beyond the impossible

No longer burdened with the heaviness of:

Hurt Because it has been EXCHANGED for fierce determination
Low Self Esteem RESTORED with the attitude of
"I'm all that and a bag of organic chips"
Unworthiness REPLACED with Deservedness and of thoughts of
"I want it all......SOCKS and DRAWALS

Shame and Guilt SUBSTITUTED with "I forgive me and I loves me some me"
And My FURY ERADICATED BY the ALL powerful
"I even forgive you"

THAT'S what TYPE OF VIBRANIUM ISH I'M ON"
WHAT ARE YOU SMOKING?

9

SHE COLD WIT IT!

Man, she cold wit it
She Bold wit it
She put her heart and soul in it
She jazzy, sophisticated and classy
Big Boned, thick and assy
She strong, clever and smart
You need to understand? That part

Throughout her life, making her mark
An octopus, swimming among you sharks
She cold with it, she bold it
She put her heart and soul in it

Striving for peace, joy and love
Time to take off these kid gloves,
Putting on armor and fighting for peace
All while praying these injustices cease
She cold wit it
She bold wit it
She put her heart and soul in it

10

FULL STEAM AHEAD

Full steam ahead and I'm coming right atcha
You put up two an I'm certain to match cha

Total it four because i did the math
Move away quickly and clear this path
You've been exposed cuz I pulled your mask
Don't you dare inquire, or even ask

Full steam ahead, can't you see the smoke?
Catch your breath quickly, before you choke
Might sound funny but this ain't no joke
Speaking right to you and all your kin folk

Full steam ahead, jump on this train
Status quo, not trying to maintain
Minding my business, you do the same
Get an umbrella. Can you stand the rain?

Full steam ahead with a good strong engine
Mind wrapped tight….waking wise decisions

Careful and cautious avoiding all collisions
Seeing so clearly cuz i finally got the vision

Full steam ahead and focused on the track
Made that bad left but I'm never going back
Directions are clear and there is no time to slack
Pay full attention and respect my black

Full steam ahead, perhaps you are the caboose
Let me know if need to cut you loose
Unless you bringing that added boost
Cuz I'll squeeze your fruit til you produce that juice

11

DIVINE PROTECTION

Divine Protection is such a beautiful thing to have
Add and subtract you do the math
Odds in your favor, the scales tip your way.
Thank you Lord, is what you will say
One of his favorites……. is who I Be
He performs wonders miraculously
One of his favorites ……..is who I Am
Just like bush that provided the Ram
A thorn of hedges he will provide
I Can't count times he has saved my hide
A thorn of hedges that he will cast
Last will become first and first will become last
All My needs he does supply,
For me there is no better ALLY
When I think of his glory, I just want to cry
For It was for my sins that he died
Divine protection is what I embrace
I need help to run this race
Divine protection is what I need

I need to listen and take heed
Divine protection is what he will provide
Love, life, peace and a good guide
Thank you Lord for my divine protection,
Introspection, grace, mercy and a sense of direction

12

THE BEST TICKET IN TOWN

Hey man I would like turn your frown upside down
Can I make you laugh? Smile? Can I get on my clown?
(or should I?)
Get dressed and change into an elegant evening gown
You want to listen to some music on the surround sound
What color tonight did you want to paint the town?

"red you say?.........did you red !!!! ...... cool "let's do it"
Shit, shower. Shave, ain't much to it
And don't forget that good cologne I bought you
You know I likes when you smell well

Concert, a movie, the theatre or a comedy show
You know the drill and how this shit go
You suited and booted cause you ready to shine
I'm still getting ready and drinking my sparkling wine
Relaxed, chillin and taking my good ol'e time

Don't get mad baby upset and fussing cause I'm not quite ready
You know I likes to pamper myself while I rock steady
All you need to do is get the confetti

(when I enter the room,)

Just clap your hands and stomp your feet
Cause I'll be dressed to the nines and this face will be beat
You in for a great time, I'm in for the good treat

Miniature golf, the park or perhaps even the zoo
Sitting in church on Sunday in our favorite pew
It's our weekend we can do whatever we want to
My job is to make you happy and please you.

Bowling, fishing, under the stars wishing
Playing some cards or barbeque in the yard
Fryin' some chicken in that good Crisco lard
Watching those Steelers' because we know they hard

This is our life and this is what us do
Sticking to our routine just me and you
Friends can come over but just only a few
But when they ass leave you know we got things to do

Clean up the house and wash those dishes
Vacuum the floor before the good kisses
Empty the bottles and take out the trash
I'll be in the bed waiting on your ass

It's all good boo because you familiar with the drill
Kick back after the show and have a good meal
Put it on you real tough with that good sex appeal
That look in your eye explains everything you feel?

Remember baby whenever you are on that sad lonely path
That I'm the best comic relief you will ever have
I'm here to turn that frown upside down
Straight up, high five and hands down
I am the best ticket in your town

13

CHECK ME, IF YOU CAN

Sometimes I wonder why I'm single with no man
Was it my mouth too much that I ran
Was it too much that I demand
Was the food I cooked too bland or was it the food I didn't cook at all
Somebody help me, cause I can't understand

I do need a king!   Someone to tell me what's the deal
Is the problem I keep it too real?
My emotions too strongly I feel
Perhaps we can discuss it over a meal

Your treat right? Or did you want me to treat?
Am I too greedy, too much do I eat?
You a vegetarian and I eat meat
You wanted me to open the door and pull out your seat

Was that the problem?

I'm open to suggestions and some good advice
But give it to me gently, not cold as ice

Don't offend me... when you check me... be nice
Cause I'll cut, chop, sauté' and slice

Oh yeah perhaps that's the problem, my ability to receive
Constructive criticism ...... I'm not totally naïve
I want a king for real, please trust and believe
Just one not in love with long hair weave
Fake eyelashes, a big butt and no common sense
How long do you think you can hold me in suspense?
I know! I know! I know...   I'm just too darn intense

But hold up a minute and let me clarify
Cause that won't shade to my ladies on the sly

I mean no offense to my girls because i was addicted to weave too
But i had to try out my own nappy hair doo
And i had too many problems with the eyelash glue
Girl! I got my issues.... And i know you do too

I know ..... I talk too much shit and don't listen enough
I'm soft and gentle and don't like all that rough stuff
You may **not** call me a bitch, a thot or a ho
Out the window all the chances will go

Being discovered by a king is such a hard feat
I'm not looking ..... Cause one day I will meet
Him,
He'll be kind, gentle, smart, funny, working, with the ability to lead
I'll follow in his footsteps, right beside him indeed
For his time and attention, I won't have to plead
We'll be there for each other in our time of need

So meanwhile, meanwhile, did i say meanwhile?
I'll check myself, and you check me if you can

Just be sure you're a real strong man
Check me right! The scrutiny I can withstand
I'll season the food and take away the bland
But faithfulness, love, respect, and trust I **will always** demand

Oh that might be the problem right there
No love no trust and full of fear
Talking crazy year after year
 a cheater, cheater, woman beater
Had a wife and couldn't keep her!
You know........a liar! Liar with his pants on fire

That's why.......and i mean........that's why

I check me.................. you check you
Unless you know what to say or what to do!
Then we can check each other, is that cool to you boo

In the bed, on the couch, in the park or under the cover
No more boyfriend! I want a husband as my lover
And certainly one I won't **have to** beg or be his mother
Just real, pure, sweet love from one to another

But check me though, if you think you can
I just might listen providing you a real man
But until then, check mate

14

NASTY NICE

I am the Queen of Nasty Nice
Have some respect or pay the price?
Precise.... I'll cut you in half in an even slice
Cut you so fast, you think I cut you twice

I will gut you like a fish
Watch you slowly dangle and twist
Give you enough time to pray and wish
Then serve your ass up on a dirty dish

I buff my Razor tongue sharp pretty often
I'm coming so hard, no blows will I soften
I'll kill you dead and you won't need a coffin
Find your ass laying up somewhere in Laughlin

I tried so hard to be nice, sweet and kind
But you played games with my mind
You ate all the melon and left me the rind
I should have left your raggedy ass behind

You didn't appreciate me when I was sweet as pie
Looked me in my face and told that lie
All while hustling that fake ass alibi
I had dreams of spitting right dead in your eye

Then, You tried to insult me.... But.... on the sly
But, I let you know in your face the reason why
I verbally abuse you until you sob
All week long like it's my full time job

You know exactly what that is all about
You made me question and have some doubt
That's why I Cut you up and spit you the fuck out

It's best to leave me alone and let me be
I'll chop you down like a cherry tree
Hatchet in your back and on one knee
That's what you'll get fucking with me

I was Compassionate, Sincere, Real and Understanding
You were Mean, Cruel, Disrespectful, Heartless and Demanding
So.....
I had to switch it up and become a ghoul
Had to take you back all the way to grammar school

To teach you a lesson you would never forget
You played out old piece of funky nasty dirty shit
Bottom of the barrel, low as you can get
 Rest assured....... I KNOW YOU GOT HIT
The Scorpio in me wouldn't let me forget

Diss me once, and I will cut you twice
I'm the Mutha fuckin' Queen of Nasty Nice

15

FULL OF SHIT AND TEARS

It's been so many years,
That I've been full of shit and tears
Scared to face fear
Pain too hard to bare
Straight feeling insincere

Had no relief for many days
Thinking this was just a phase
Unable to count the ways
Confused in a haze

So

I sit…. I squat…I squeeze…. I pout
But nothing ever comes out
Still left with the shame and doubt
My emotions must i live without
What is all this misery about?

Imagine this..sad twist
I can't even count the years
I've been so full of shit and tears

Not sure how long it has been since i cried
Tears dried
Tongue-tied
When folks lied
Hurt pride
Friends died

Still not a drop
When did my emotions stop?
Stiffled
Constipation obstruction
Interruption of life flow
Where did my shit and tears go?

Lord, please clear my colon
Cleanse my soul
I just want to be whole

I desperately miss me
Wish my tears would flow free
Crystal clear so I can find me

Yet I'm still left
 full of shit and tears

16

SOLD A DREAM

A man will sell you a helluva dream
Make you believe in love and everything
Tell you, *"I'll make you happy baby"*
"For real, this is a promise and not a maybe"

"I got your back, no need to worry"
"Let's take our time no need to hurry"

"Girl, where have you been all my life"
"I been looking for someone like you to wife"
Now you at the store buying rice
Perfume for you and for him old Spice
Then he say
"You're so smart, pretty and just my type"
Pump it up hard with a lot of hype
Waiting to pick you but you ain't quite ripe

"Girl you look so good, nice and sweet"
"Taste delicious and you good to eat"
"I am whole you make my life complete"

"Come sit right here baby, this your seat"
"With another woman you won't ever compete"
"I love you girl more than life itself"
Place you on a pedestal high on a shelf
"I'll protect you and keep you in good health"
"When we're not together baby, I'm not myself"

"Baby girl, I care for you like no other"
"Me and you together forever, my lover"
"Kiss me girl, not once but twice"
"You love me baby? Ain't this nice"

"I long for you, my love is strong"
"Loving you is right, I feel no wrong"

"You're my destiny, my lover, my all and all"
"Why you think every day I call?"
Chipping away at your hardened wall
He selling you that dream until you fall

Deep in love with all your heart
You didn't expect it to be torn apart
He was good and did his best
He had me, I fell hard, I Had to confess
But life goes on nevertheless

A dream deferred, postponed, delay
Men get the side eye now when they say **HEY**
A snake can say Hi, They don't all **HISS**
Next time it's the bullshit I won't miss

Learn to recognize, they slick on the prowl
Learn to discern like an old wise owl
Cause many men are scandalous and fowl

So Say goodbye with a beautiful smile
Don't be afraid to throw in that towel.

I was sold a dream but I didn't have to buy it

17

PROFILE

Girl, he did not "Sell You a Dream"
You just fit the Profile
You could never love a man that did time in the Pen
They're too damaged, wounded, and empty within.
They too scared, soulless, bent and broken
Left for dead with nothing to hope in.
First law of nature is always to survive
Heart dead, no pumps can revive
That Hard core mentality, full of reality
that no one ever gave a fuck about him.
Then came YOU
But it's too late, that hate been set in stone
Spent way too much time alone.
On them hard ass cots, with fucked up thoughts.
It was like fighting a dog over the same bone.
That nigga will chew YOU
To eat to the heart of his own pain
Inflict hurt trying to maim YOU.
Sis you know where I'm going with this.
He did not Sell You a Dream,

You just fit the Profile.
Learn how to peep game, they look the same
He saw your heart and took aim.
He Learned how to hunt for a great one,
at gate one; stepped up his game to take one.
Girl, he did not Sell You a Dream
You just fit the MF'n Profile

18

AFTER THE CLUB AND LONELY

After the club and lonely
Damn no one to bone me
Called one, called two
What's a horny sista to do?

Read, Sleep or eat
I ain't got no meat to beat
So close your eyes and sleep
Wake up tomorrow and repeat

This is a lonely feeling
You fuckers be illin'
I'm sleepy, horny, hungry and tired
All you muthafuckas fired!

19

HE CAME ON SO STRONG

Like gang busters, He was as boisterous and as exciting as a Fire work extravaganza! I'm talking Big Bang Boom
He made his presence known and his intentions clear
He introduced himself and told me who he was, what he was about and how much we had in common,
He proceeded to inform me of who he thought I was... because he could read me, read my energy and he knew what I needed in my life
He thought that we would be great together, He thought I was attractive, He loved my voice and said it sounded familiar and comfortable to him
He was clear that he wanted me and I needed someone like him
He announced " You are strong and independent
and a whole lot of woman to handle"
He confessed, that I Might scare some men, might intimidate others.... but not him
He declared that he was equipped to do the job, and was the right one for it
He insisted that I had never met a man in my life like him before
And that he read my book and couldn't wait to read more

He assumed that he knew me in a way like no other
that no man would take the time to understand me the way he would
He called six times a day and sang a familiar song, one
of my favorites
He asked, could I stand rain? could I weather storm? Cause
they would come
He had me thinking about a whole New Edition
He presented with such inner confidence, an all-consuming
vision and a burning desire
He was so persistent, incessant, tenacious, unrelenting,
and contagious
Somehow, I knew he wouldn't be able to keep that up,
how could anyone?
He came on so strong that I knew he couldn't keep that pace
He tried to run a marathon knowing he was only capable
of a 5k race
But what I didn't expect was for him to come on THAT strong
But go out THAT weak, I mean like a used tea bag that once
produced strong black fragrant tea
He changed from a firework show to the sparkler the little kids
hold in their hands-on the 4th of July
He came in like a lion and went out like a lamb
He turned from A torrential thunderous tsunami to
barely a rainy mist
He was a Noah Ark flood that turned into a poor man puddle
He was so big and black, his presence so strong… now he's invisible
even under a microscope, I couldn't find him or a needle
in a haystack
Three paramount questions I ask myself
Am I surprised? Do I care? Will I live to tell about it?
No, I'm not surprised, nope I couldn't care less and of course I'll
live to tell about it. That's exactly what I'm doing now, you see, he
remembers I'm a writer and that's one of the things he
liked that about me, you see,

All life experiences help me grow and provide good subject matter for a good ole' poem or short story perhaps, or maybe even a chapter in my book.
But What will be his story? What say he?
Reflect with introspect then ask himself the BIG WHY's
Why did I try to get this woman when I didn't know what I would do with her?
Why did I open my mouth when my silence should have stayed golden?
Why did I approach her when I had no follow through?
Why did I not just admire her from a far distance?
Why did I sell wolf tickets when I had no show?
Why did I suggest places I know we wouldn't go?
Why did I promise a rose garden when I had no yard?
Why did I try to play games when I had no card?
Why did I pretend that I could do the most?
Why did I brag and boast when I had no toast?
I know, I know...I know..... He knew better all along
To tried to sell a dream and sing a song
He knew to contact her from the start was wrong
I don't know WHY he introduced himself and came on so strong

20

IT'S BEEN REAL

It's been real about what we had
But has everything been said?
You love me. You miss me. You want me back
Is it only because I'm great in the sack?

Was it about me or about the Intimacy
Or what you thought about fearlessly
Was it real true love or a joke?
Maybe it was the words you often spoke

That convinced me to love, trust and believe
Or words that were meant to deceive,
To manipulate my mind, my heart and soul
Was supposed to last as we grow old

Your words were often forceful and bold
But as time passed, those words turned cold

So I'm out, I'm gone, so long, GOODBYE
I'm sick of all your fuckin lies

It was real for a little while
But now it's time to close your file

Due to the fact that you can't commit
Moreover, I'm sick of your bullshit!
It's been REAL

21

F__K BOY

Hey F__K   Boy,
Why you lying when the truth will do
You scheming because it suits you

You are an old man playing a childish game
Missed the toilet seat, that's how fucked up is your aim
So many excuses they all sound the same
I'm no longer interested and you're the blame

You too old to be still be a fuckboy
Parading around like a man toy
No meat, no consistency no flavor, ... you're like soy
I will never compromise my joy for a fuck boy

Void of substance, character and style
Too much aggravation this could take a while
But I'll just smile and read your rights to remain a young, old fool
Playing games like you think it's still cool
Ain't that the same shit you did in high school?

Give them just enough so that they become complacent
Your lack of concern is too obvious and blatant
Keep them in line so they don't know the rotation
Call them when you think they are becoming impatient
All while picking and choosing their replacement

No call or no text in over a week
That's disrespectful, we don't need to speak
Your lack of attention speaks volumes to me
I'm definitely not blind, I can clearly see

You don't back burner me, until you get time
I'm already writing my next poetry line
Boy bye, go to sleep, wake up and try again
Next time you might appreciate a real friend

I'm not dumb fuck boy. I'm smarter than that
I'm not your everyday neighborhood rat
Chase you? NO, NO... I would never do that
I'm a just hip you to a well-known fact

Fuck boys come a dime a dozen
Just like a pie and a cake in the oven
I thought you were better with high potential
Determined to succeed and become influential

I have no hard feelings and no expectation
With you I don't want no type of relation
Just to let you know I see through you clearly
I hope one day that you miss me dearly
Bye fuck boy

2 2

DISILLUSIONED

I created in my head my very own illusion
My mind and heart filled often with confusion
If it's not a real or true.......Then it's a fixed delusion
Reality sets in and serves you a conclusion

As I think about where I thought we were headed
On the road, on a journey of togetherness, you and I
No more wondering why and no more little white lies

Not realizing, I was on the road to nowhere all by myself
Just me and I...... and no one else
Your hand slipped so easily from mine
I should have been wiser and taken more time

As briefly as you held my interest you quickly let it go
I guess it wasn't meant to be so
But why wasn't I the first to know

I found myself trapped in the thought of what it could have been
Falling in love but you were never really all in

More lost on the thought of what it should have been...
more than that of what is
All I felt was.....He was going to be mine... and I was gone be his,

I had this real strong incredible desire
To look in your eyes and see that fire
Because it was you that I was starting to admire
But it was my hopes and dreams that made me my own liar

I had big dreams but too many unspoken words
Reading between the lines of words I hadn't even heard
Misled, thrown off course, thinking grown men don't hint
They don't leave you wondering where the hell they went

I saw you through one single rose colored glass
All the dreams and hopes I thought we could surpass
There was just one important question, I forgot to ask
And that was.......Do you think that you and I will last?

I became overzealous, eager, so I just jumped the gun
It's my fault, I thought you were the one
On that first date.....we had so much fun
I was ready to hold hands on the beach under the sun
But it was Dinner for two but future plans only for one

In retrospect, I laugh at myself but it isn't even funny
I was ready to call this man my honey
He was not interested in me but focused on making money

Or so he said

My care or concern no longer does he get

We never had the chance to even make a commitment
I wish you well and I have no resentment
Focus back on me and my own contentment
So I'm out his way and back focused on me
The only safe place that I need to be
The only one I can count on to make me happy...... is me
I'm sad because he was just too damn blind to see
But the illusion didn't come from him that came from me
So I have to woman up and take full responsibility

This time I sold myself a dream A full on delusion
But in the end I always get me a poem and a good conclusion

23

I CAN'T MAKE MYSELF CRY

I can't make myself cry…I don't even wonder why………I just sigh
I been through this shit many times before
With your black sorry ass at my door
Lying, stumbling and often drunk
Smelling like Kush or maybe skunk

Sorry man, NOPE….. I can't take no more
Get the fuck away from my front door
With all that bullshit, bout you sorry
Tell that mess to your uncle Charlie
I can't make myself cry! I just can't do it
Not a sniff, not a tear, damn nigga you blew it
You had too many chances with me
Time to open my eyes and face reality
Can't make myself Cry, Not even one time
Especially over a dude that ain't got a dime.
Anything else to say? Put it in a rhyme
I can't make myself cry

24

DON'T LET THE SMOOTH TASTE FOOL YOU

You know how those sweet honey dripping words will make you melt
Baby, baby, hey baby every single word felt
Be careful and play the cards you've been dealt

Slightly whispered words used to manipulate your mind
Watch out for them, they are a special kind
 will separate your body from your heart
Some bullshit designed from the start
 play you straight like tattoo art

Multi-facted ink lines intertwined
Poke you slowly a million times
Blurry lines hard to define
Have you drinking cheap wine

Don't let the smooth taste fool you:

Break you down and have you grinning

How you think he stay winning
A plot and a plan from the beginning

He will eat your p___y until your knees quiver
Break you down until you deliver
Leave you so cold until you shiver
Shed many tears to fill a river

Don't let the smooth taste fool you
He will make a monkey out of you
and leave you at the zoo,
Call you later and say what happened boo?
I got lost and couldn't find you,

These fools out here ain't no joke
How and why you think i stay woke
Ain't nothing cute about being out here broke
Don't you fall for the okie doke

He looking all fly in your shit
Now your pockets full of lint
Now you short on your bills
Now how the fuck do you really feel?

They will try to get you for all you're worth
Make you feel like you've been cursed
Make you reject your birth

Break you down like a double barrel shot-gun
Game over...no more fun
Take all you have until you have none
Watch and see how fast he run

Don't let the smooth taste fool ya:
All they want is your ass and your moolah
That's why I'm here to school ya

Moolah...that's your green, your cheese your hard earned buck
Gave him some ass, now your double fucked
You all in love and now you stuck
Left trying to figure out what's up?

You done fucked up and let the smooth taste fool ya!
Don't let it happen to you again.

25

PAINFULLY DROWNING

When did my life become so miserable so complicated?
I can't remember the day I began to hate it

What happened to eat, sleep, work, family, friends and some occasional sex
A small argument with the ex, nothing complex

I remember when things were so simple, easy and fair
Now I feel empty, unsure, discouraged and bare
You were my breathe and I was your air
Now all I feel is hopelessness and despair

My heart can't take anymore tears
Disgusted, angry and living in fear
I long for the days of yesteryear

You have turned my life upside down
That I no longer know which way is up
Am I coming or am I going?
 I'm lost and I don't know

Now I feel every burden on my back,
Stuck like a hostage, tortured and trapped

Every grey hair you have given me I have not earned
Horrible memories I can't wait to burn,
For my peace of mind, I yearn
For my happiness to return
I can no longer recognize joy
Like a thief in the night it was stolen
So many tears, eyes closed shut and swollen

How did this happen for I never seen it coming
You chasing and me running
I remember the days you were stunting
Now there is no growth!

Your destruction has crippled me
Blinded me, I can no longer see
All I know is misery

A change must come or I will run
Into a land without you
Because this is too hard,
I can't keep watching

26

IS IT REAL OR MEMOREX

Is it real or is it Memorex
Is it wise to mess with your Ex
Been through this story line before
The after effects, I still feel sore
From the emotional beating that I took
Time for a Brand new outlook
Technology has advanced from pager to text
But my concerns are what's next
The same old story, old movie and drama
Is it time for a comma?
Maybe a period or a question mark
Because I refuse to remain in the dark
About this situation, it cause too much aggravation
And much more dedication that I care to give,
I'm just trying to live
Real or Memorex, should I even consider the ex
I am Tired of contemplating and wondering what's next
Real or Memorex
Perhaps we'll just have sex

27

THIS AIN'T YOUR HEART

This ain't your heart not even your Pussy
You punked out fool just like a big sissy
It won't hit you now until you miss me
You tried to play games and even diss' me

There will come a day that you will ask when
Where the fuck Kim been?
She ain't called to check on a brother
You know why nigga, she with another

You couldn't get it together and be a real man
So it shouldn't be hard for you to understand
That a woman like me can pick and choose
And certainly not a fool that prefers the booze

I'm tired of your shit and sick of your ass
Enough is enough I'm done at last
No more chance or another pass
Go back to school and take a class
Because you need to know

This ain't your pussy not even your heart
This was some bullshit doomed from the start

28

WHEN THE HOT BURNING LOVES TURNS LUKEWARM

When the hot burning loves turns to lukewarm
I feel like a dark cloud in a rolling thunderstorm
I wonder when did the love die and transform
How did i become the victim of him scorn?
Lights, camera, action, now its time for me to perform

Our spicy love was once a blazing like a roaring fire
Hot passion, caressing deep dark desire
Of that good love, I thought I would never get tired
It was you….. And only you…. That i strongly admired

Our love was deep, sensual, exciting… a sense of thrill
Not like this did i imagine i could ever feel
I pledged my love solid and sealed the deal
I just didn't know what time would reveal

Our love was so hot like a flame in a candle
I guess i was just too much for you to handle
So, you exhausted the fire on the wick
And left me with a dry ass candle stick
I thought about a good punch right in your lip
Or let the wax drip on your nuts and your d_ _k

Our love was strong together and totally complete
Every time I saw you my heart skipped a beat
I was so nervous at times I couldn't even eat
We was winning clearly not a chance for defeat
But of course, you fucked it up
Because you're you……. That's what you do
Then you want to think about it and   cry boo hoo

Too late you burned this hot flame out
I don't care how much you sit around and pout
I tried to explain to you what love and compromise was about
"but i love you" is what now what you want to shout"

Now you want to make me an offer I can't refuse
It's you again that you want me to choose?
You didn't listen when I sang the blues
So, guess what old lover it's…. Me you lose

Next time be sweet, loving, kind but oh no you were rude
If you had been nicer you'd still be my dude
So now my love is faded gone, into the night
Next time listen and learn and have some insight
With your next woman… I hope your future is bright
Cause you have exhausted my flame and my light

That's what happens when the burning love turns lukewarm

29

YOU LOVING ME IS EASY?

Confusion sets in as I try to understand
What is it that he is really trying to say
What thought is he trying to convey?
Perhaps another mind game he's trying to play

He wants to get in my mind and my thighs
He wants to take me on a sexual high
Lift me up and encourage me to fly
Too bad it's all based on a lie

So, which one of us is easy to love?
I'm inclined to believe it has to be me
But he is arrogant enough to believe that it is he
Perhaps we must just wait and see

So direct and usually very clear
Let's me know that he wants me near
He blames my avoidance on fear
But, nope.......I refuse to shed a tear

Me afraid? Never that
Perhaps it's where you live at
You think I'm the ball and you're the bat
You won't walk over me like a floor mat

30

INEVITABLE

It was almost certain that you and I would meet
The casino, a concert, down the street
Introduced by a co-worker and a mutual friend
You realized immediately, I was a Godsend

You said, Baby, You are the one, as you looked deep into my eyes
Knowing full well you were winning the prize
And my love for you came to you as no surprise

It was certain to happen, totally inescapable
Trying to impress me, you were more than capable
Rough times and bad patches were hard to avoid
Sometimes I even thought you had taken steroid

You got on my nerves and I got on yours
The relationship was becoming more like a chores
Understanding, learning and thriving is what we needed
Determined to be together and not be defeated

It's been a long tumultuous year and a half

Most of the fights, I hope are in the past
Hard to figure out what lies ahead
Perhaps some traveling and more fun in the bed
Exciting and adventurous I'm waiting to see
Pre-ordained, necessary and meant to be
Handmade and woven, we fit to a T
Who thought it could ever happen to me?
And the look in his eyes still full of glee

It's in the bag, it's in the cards
Can't wait for you to grow me a garden in our yard
Sun shining, rain, fog or good weather
It is Inevitable that we belong together

It was a Pre-determined path by the force of love
We fit smugly together like a glove

It was Inevitable

31

HYPNOTIZED BY LIES

Swing the pendulum so I sleep
Transfixed in thought deep
Wake up and weep

Hypnotized by lies
Weeping eyes ~ She cries

Pull the bunny out the hat
Trick mirror she fat
Wondering where the sandwich at
No magic bullet….bat

Self-conscious invaded
Memories faded
Left jaded

Hypnotized, hurt and hit
Now the clothes don't fit
In the audience you sit
Sprinkled with fairy dust

32

LOST

Lost in thought, time and space
Feeling the need to leave this place
Too many thoughts in my head....Erase

My own head, full of woe
Where can I run, Where can I go?

I'm Lost, to thinking and feeling
My mind keeps reeling.

Out of control and beyond belief
I'm Overdue for some relief

Stressed out, worried, I can't sleep
Plenty fears and tears, I weep.
I'm overwhelmed, this shit is too deep

I grasp my head and wonder why?
I Grip my heart and let out a sigh

A scream, of terror and sadness
How did   I get caught up in the madness?
I am lost and don't know what to do
Not many choices, only one or two

Wondering Will it work, or is it enough?
All I know is I am tired of this stuff

I need some peace in my life
Not my heart torn out with a knife

I am lost with you
I am Lost without you
I am lost in time, thought, and space

33

OLD NEW SHIT

How do you begin some old new shit
Maybe we shouldn't, cuz that apples been bit
It could be right or wrong or a perfect fit
If done right, this shit could be on hit

Perhaps it is too late... and our time has passed
But what can I do?......... This fool all on my ass
It feels good and it feels right at times
In fact, it make me want to just bust this rhyme

As I spit this shit with conviction and spice
I'm wondering if he can be nice twice
To me that is and not to another
If not.... COOL...... on to the next brother

But he handsome, nice eyes, good teeth with a big stick and all
But what about that heart, what if the sucker small

Damn... too much thinking....quite a bit
Should I wait on this old new shit?

Or should I just quit lickety split?
How do I begin to wrap my mind round this old new shit

34

4 of CLUBS

I WANT A King, No more 4 of clubs, 9 of hearts
or Jack of Diamonds,
They talk real fast, low-key rhyming
They truth not in em, they steady be lying
Commitment, love, honor, trust the words be flying

Out they mouth and under our heart
As the love and loyalty begin to depart
You sure, this some shit you want to start?

Lied about work, what they have, and what they do
One even lied, said he was sick with the flu
I caught his ass the same day in San Diego at the zoo,
With a cute new boo with a nice hair doo

I said OH "You got well fast, you looking good"
With another woman is where he stood
Healed real nice, good and quick
Man this one thought he was slick
Unaware, He just missed a swift kick to his dick,

But I'm not that chick

(Well, not no more)

He was by her side, he and scared to move
Thought I would mess up his groove

He was holding hands and smiling
He thought he was clowning,
As I stood there frowning

(For one second)

Not I said the cat! Where my man at?
Behind me to stood, tall and looking good
I said, Yall have fun and a good day
As, we turned to walked away
I winked my eye and threw up the Deuces'
Love, peace and smooches

Then suddenly, I began to grin
Realizing he did not win
No more 4 of clubs, 9 of hearts or Jack of Diamond
The heart of this King, Is where I'm climbing
(Tonight)

35

I STILL WANT A KING

I want a sure fire bona fide king
Not one that suggests I buy my own ring
Not one who cheats and does his own thing
But one whose love doesn't hurt or sting

I still believe in love and a good strong relationship
Spending time alone, time together not joined at the hip
My bags are packed, I'm focused …… I'm ready for the trip
Hand holding, hugging, a big juicy lick on his tip
I'll hold it tightly to make sure it don't slip
A walk on the white sandy beach and a nice good sip
Butt asshole naked and ready to skinny dip

I want righteous, dependable, loving man…. A king
one who has something to the table to bring

One i can honor, respect, admire and trust
Being in love with him also is definitely a must

I need more than just a touch and horny lust
Something interesting, a good topic for us to discuss

I want a king in whose eyes i can look in and feel proud
Announce to the world in front of a crowd
Introduce my king and say" look a here at this scrumptious deal"
No more low budget dates or no more low budget meals
A whole lot of my dreams he would certainly fulfill
He would even speak truth and keep it all real
All these years of dating and many years have past
It was never a lack of fellows trying to get at this ass
Just liars, cheaters, unemployed boys, none that could last
They was just so full of shit so i put they ass on blast

Promptly cuss they ass out and let them know I'm not that fool
I had to take at least ten of em' back to elementary school
Trying to get over, take advantage or play a stupid game
I had to let em know that Kim and Kacee is one in the same
And they can go back to hell from whence they came

I don't really want anyone for real go to hell
But I know one or two had to come from somebody's jail
Writing all that bullshit from within a two men cell
Hoping it would be foolproof and unable to fail
Cause he already had one that paid his previous bail
just waiting to spring that dumb shit on the next unsuspecting female

Yup, I still want a king
But I'm not settling for any ole' thing

36

HIM AND ME 4 LIFE AND THEN SOME

Him and me for life and then some
Wondering if you can still make me cum
Hard and fast or soft "n" slow
Please just let it curl my toe

Him and me for Life and then some more
Sex on the bed, then on the floor
Making your way home to me
Can you imagine the possibility?
Hold up man.....Just wait and see

Speak of a Love Real Solid and Strong
Feels so right... It can't go wrong
Wasn't that the name of that song?
Never mind. Fuck that.... Is the Dick still long?

AW shit got me thinkin' bout my dude
Lights, candles, cause I'm in the mood

Best believe he is in the zone
Baby... what time you say you get home?

HIM AND ME 4 LIFE AND THEN SOME

37

It IS AMAZING To ME ENGLISH AND SPANISH

It is amazing to me that after all these years you can alleviate my fears and make me think about love in a brand new way

Me sorprende que después de todos estos años puedas aliviar mis miedos y hacerme pensar sobre el amor de una manera completamente nueva.

It is amazing to me that I love your voice and the choice words you say that make my day happy, completed and filled with thought of you all day

Me parece increíble que amo tu voz y las palabras de tu elección que hacen que mi día sea feliz, completo y lleno de pensamientos sobre ti todo el día

It is amazing to me that when I hear your laughter, it makes me smile and fills my heart with unspeakable joy

Me sorprende que cuando escucho tu risa, me hace sonreír y llena mi corazón de una alegría indescriptible

It is amazing to me that you possess that kind of swagger and edge that makes me want to pledge my allegiance to you always

Es increíble para mí que poseas ese tipo de confidencia que me hace querer prometer mi lealtad a ti siempre

It is amazing to me that you knocked me off so quick, before I had the chance to cough up too many reasons of why we should not be

Es sorprendente para mí que me hayas desconectado tan rápido, antes de tener la oportunidad de explicar muchas razones por las que no deberíamos estarlo

It is amazing to me that I love you with such strong intensity, that I I have the propensity to make you a priority in my life forever

Es increíble para mí que te amo con tanta intensidad, que tengo la propensión de hacerte una prioridad en mi vida para siempre

It is amazing to me!
Is it amazing to you

¡Es asombroso para mí!
Es asombroso para ti

38

ALL I WANTED TO DO IS SKIP TO THE LOU WITH MY BOO

All I wanted to do was skip to the Lou with my Boo
So we got together and became my dude
Within 3 months, he was rude….Crude

I was beyond despair
It was something I couldn't repair

All I Wanted to do was Skip to the Lou with my Boo
All he wanted to do was be right
Mornin' noon and night
Fuss, argue and fight
Tunnel got so dark I could barely see light
Can you understand a sistah's plight?
You see, He is the type of man that would
Argue with his right hand when he masturbate

All I wanted to do was skip to the Lou with my Boo
He didn't understand that my feelings were important to me
Nor how his words stung like a bee
I tried hard to make him see
But the only thought he had was of HE

He was smart, intelligent and dumb, all at the same time
To take my advice would have been a crime

So he talked and he talked and he talked some more
I finally put his black ass out my door
From behind the door, he continued to squawk
Like an old dried up dusty hawk'
Get away, Run, Fly or walk
Get off my jock. Tick Tock
You've been cock blocked

Cry sigh and deny, it was like having a needle in my eye
All I wanted to do was skip to the Lou with my Boo
Next time
I think I'll walk

39

NOT SURE ABOUT WHAT MAY HAPPEN

Not sure about what may happen
But I can be the lieutenant, if you can be the captain
Is time to get off my throne and let a new king reign supreme
Cuz that's always been my dream
I'll rub some cream on the back of my old school lover
Especially one that I recently rediscovered
Are u Sneakin, peaking, and honey dipping?
Are you still in the streets straight money flipping?
Have you gotten it together and making better choices?
Gotten a job and filled out some invoices?
Man you know you were out there man on them streets
And I ain't trying to have history repeat
You see, many years have passed and things are brand new
Why are campaigning to be my boo?
Well you be strong patient and true
Can you still make it do what it do?
We will be out in the open for all the world to know

Man, you sure you ready for the show?
Like I said:
I'm not sure about what may happen
But I'll be the lieutenant! CAN you be the captain?
But SEE I wrote this poem many years ago
So I had to update and add this flow
He was not a captain nor a lieutenant
I'm sorry and regret that I ever got in.

40

GOOD BROTHERS

This poem is for the good, strong, loving, kind brothers
The tallest tree in the forest among all other brothers
romantic, sensual, sexual, you know.... The good lover brothers
It took some time to realize and rediscover
That there are some real genuine good brothers

They are just a different type of dude
Self-assured, confident and very rarely rude
It's their woman that they love and include
He will respect her peace and her solitude
In return, she is faithful, sweet and has a good attitude

You are a good brother, a real solid type of man
Takes care of his family the best he can
He keeps it real so that his woman understands
His expectations and their life plans
He pays her attention, so she don't have to demand

Good smart brother with a good head on his shoulders
Compliments his woman every day as she gets older

He waits for the right moment just in case he has to scold her
Take her in his arms because he knows it's time to hold her

Kiss her eyelids softly as she begins to cry
Trying to figure it out and understand why
He will Tell her the truth and have no need to lie
Kiss her on the lips gently in the morning as he says goodbye

Good brother, Good brothers there are not many like you
Hard working, intelligent, courageous and insightful
Looking at you she gets more than an eyeful
You're a pillar of strength and always have your mind full

You are a Special man and you stand out in a crowd
You speak volumes without even talking loud
Your voice is calming but you make things clear
You pull her close and always keep her near

She's Close to your heart......she is your right arm
You funny and handsome and you full of that good charm
You protect and shield her from any and all harm

Good brother, good brother you are one in a million
She will Fall In love with you with real true feelin'
You are Worth your weight in gold, I say perhaps a trillion

Passionate about life and you're such a great leader
Love and respect her, you won't ever try to beat her
You Lift your family up with strong, meaningful prayers
Multifaceted and complex, you have so many layers
You Got your own mind right and won't listen to naysayers

You are ambitious, goal oriented yet still down to earth
Destined to be somebody but that was determined from your birth

You are loyal to your family and will always protect your turf
Demand your respect because you know your worth

Good brother, Good brother, good brother
I honor you........ I salute you
I revere, love, trust and respect you
It's my privilege to write this poem and re- introduce you

I acknowledge you for the kings that you are
You are exceptional, well put together and outstanding   By far
A good brother, well it is just who the heck you are

Shout out to the good brothers everywhere!

41

NEGRO PLEASE NEVER EVER GET RIPPED OPEN

I went and seen this movie, Birth of a Nation
Emotions ran so high. I feel like I need a vacation
Trying to get those images out of my head
Of Black folks and white folks lying dead

Thinking about the pain that my ancestors endured
Imagining their thoughts as they approached the shore

No clue or idea of what they were in for
Stripped down butt all the way to the core

Savagely beaten Flesh torn away from the skin
Raped, tortured, taken away from my kin
Back sewed up neatly stitch by stitch
young bucks show bravery and never flinch
Sopping up the blood to see the wounds clear
 wondering how much more is there to bare

All while dreaming of a day and a life of freedom
Scared to leave master, cause you think you need em'
Stripped of their heritage and in a new land
And Master requests for sex On demand

Avoiding the lash was always a daily goal
To keep your family safe and maintain your soul
Thoughts of death was better than growing old
But ain't no time for that there is clothes to fold

So they do what they can daily to get by
Ever so careful not to look the over seer In the eye
Songs, dances and hymns provided as refuge
Disguised cleverly to throw off and confuse

The sound and beat of the drum in the air
Knowing it was time to act and no longer fear
Revolt. Revolution the time draws near
Death, destruction. No more time for despair

Old negro preacher, led an uprise
Using Biblical passages as his he disguise
60 slaves joined together by the end
But 200 more died as master struck revenge

Stay woke Fast forward it is now to 2016
ask yourself really, what does it all mean?

Same ole crap, Different day with familiar hate
This time disguised as make America GREAT

42

MAD

We Killin' the game
Is that why they killing us?
They can't understand that we don't trust
Cause we are aware they would rather bust

First, shoot to kill, and ask no questions
no de-escalation, no Taser, no suggestions,
no hesitations, No justification,
Just a simple lack of dedication
and a ready-made statement of
"he was resisting" neatly stored on a shelf of
alibis

"I have never been more afraid for my life,"
So I took his,
I Never had one thought of his kids

The wheels of justice, slowly they will turn

meanwhile its's his reputation, that we must burn
demean, disgrace and dehumanize
We will make them believe horrendous lies

Did he have a gun? "OH, I don't remember"
Cut him down because he was a contender
We got Flowers for his mom that you can send her
extend some sympathy like a fake pretender

Blues, despair. I don't really Care
One less nigga that's sharing my air
What? You thought that I would be fair?
Respect and dignity with them I should share?

We Killin' the game
Is that why they killing us?
afraid, angry Mad at our success
Mad because we make requests
Mad we passed so many tests
Mad this some shit they got to address
Mad that our feelings we must express
Mad when we organize and protest
Mad cause they sinful and transgress
Mad cause when stressed, we still stay blessed
Mad cause you have to wear a bullet proof vest
Mad is why you shot him in his chest?

Yeah, we killin the game
That is why they killing us
They wish we would have stayed in the back of that bus.
If we had... Do you think there would be this fuss?
But making progress was a must

Too bad they just couldn't adjust
But yeah, that is why they killin' us

They Mad

43

BLACK QUEEN IN THE EYE OF THE STORM

It does not feel like the time to reform
I'm a Black Queen in the eye of the storm.
Gather resource it's time to transform

This one sided battle, this disregard
Time to come together and boggard
Demand our rights and our respect
No longer willing to be just a suspect

As I watch my kind, struggle and die
Watching them tell lie after lie
With the smugness of eating apple pie
Realizing they are not an ally

Waving their rights as they step on ours
Taking our lives days,   minutes and hours
Fed up, cried out and tired
Why none of these mofo's every get fired

This mess is hard to see and hear
Watching my own live in fear
Shedding the same tear, year after year.
When will it stop When will it cease
Why mofo's can't leave in peace

 Nah, this does not feel like the time to reform
I'm a Black Queen in the eye of the storm.

44

JUNETEENTH

June 19th, 1865 is the date the slaves in America were freed
Not the last of the trouble as they were just beginning indeed
Juneteenth, is a celebration of emancipation started in the Confederate South Freedom,
Joy and excitement pouring from every mouth

Well not every mouth, there were those that were upset
 It was on our labor they could no longer benefit and bet
Independence and Justice was finally being met
No more were we just property to own or sublet

The process was slow and it took over two years
Word travelled slowly and so did all the fears
Resistance was high and the war was not easily won
Danger and violence, cannons and guns

Freedom only applied to those slaves by union lines
It took a long time for states to define
While Confederates continued to fight for more time

Emancipation papers? You thought they wanted to sign?
Slavery was well crafted it was a malicious design
They wanted slavery enforced..... Not for it to decline

They wanted to own folks and have free labor
Upset that one day we would be their neighbor
They began to corrupt the law to an all-time low
These suckers came up with something called "Jim Crow"

A Negro is three/fifths a person How did they do that math?
But it shows us clearly how we got on this path
Given the information the day after it passed
Stacking the odds against us so that we would be last

Segregation, Lynching, racism, redlining and inferior education
Signed, sealed, delivered in legal documentation
Signed with a feathered pen with no hesitation
"You can't vote NEGRO you don't meet the rules of registration"

Sharecropping for old master was only a temporary move
That was until we learned to find our groove

Independence, skill, bravery and courage
Uplifting, sharing no words to discourage
Building, growing, establishing a new community
Black pride, peace, wealth, hard work and unity
They continued to kill with blatant impunity
Deeply wounded ....we need some immunity
Determined to stay strong and pursue our opportunity

Black Wall Street was our first real prosperous town
But of course, they got jealous and mad and burned it down
To the ashes and to the dust it burned to the floor
Murdering rotten savages down to their evil core

On NEGROES they staged a full blown war
Pushed to the limits, we can't take no more

Today, my people are focused, determined to build and grow
But we Putting you on notice, just so you know
We demand our rights, our justice and peace
Because we will never ever forget **JUNETEENTH**

45

POMONA, CA

Age 12, Moved from Pittsburgh PA to the heart of Pomona CA.
Daring, Determined and Destined and to have my way,
Same friends I had since back in the day

Sintown, The Islands, Patty Track, Village, Kellogg and Ghost Town
12th Street, Cherryville, Barjud, Happy Town
You know these places cuz it's all where it went down
Low riders, bikes, and skates and "C" walking is how we got around

The Angelo's, CV's, the Tiki's and Murchison
On them streets wasn't nothing but purchasing
You name it, they had It, nothing but trouble
If you had enough money they would make it double

TMack, Rob and Jessie, Percy Mack and the homeboy Drak
All the homeboys hung together in the same track
Chasing girls, gambling; bet one or two had a sac
Golf Hats, leather Coats, Stacey Adams and slacks
Ain't hard to figure why they called themselves Macks

Ganesha, Garey, and Pomona High
The Girls from each side were all so fly
Stone cold brick houses we was Bad to the bone
One cold look and we had you in the zone
We had cheerleaders, girl jocks, and some even gang bang
But everybody was cool and did their own thang
Lolo, Pearlie and Gail paper Thin
I never joined Blood or Crip and I never got jumped in
But I liked them rough, tough, handsome and with good money
Waving from across the street, "How you doing honey?"

There were Hustler's, Players and the Pimps
The square dude, the Wanna Be's and the Simps'

Entrepreneurs, professionals, Rappers, Poets and Bosses
Pomona had some winners but we took a lot of losses

My sister Loni, my steady right hand any my true best friend
Together since day one… always trying to win
She trustworthy, loyal, fun and always on my side
I Love her, respect her and my feelings I can't hide

At Ganesha I hung out with, Pam, Angela, Leslye, ARNessa and Ahna, Soni, Patricia Killibrew, both Diana's, Nita and Tanya
 Some fights, fussing, drama but it ended better than it started
Made up and became friend's way before we parted

You Went to Park West if you had trouble or got behind
Cut class… at Kennedy Park… trying to get that grind
Looking for a hot girl one you had to find
Dropping some Bullshit to get in her mind
             BUT
Some of us good girls liked bad boys in the hood
Convinced ourselves ya'll was just misunderstood

Academy, Farrington, Carlton, and Concord
Partying at the Phipps' house on Avalon was all good

Towne, Mission, Garey and the known Holt Stroll
Way before hoes was even swinging on a pole
We didn't know then that dope make you lose your soul
Put yourself back together and make yourself whole

Kwan's, Donahoo's, Ox Burger, and Shakey's bunch a lunch
Be Careful at the party not to drink that spiked punch
Homegrown, SESAMEA, and Columbian Gold made you munch
Pay more attention and respect your first hunch

Won a 70's costume party at the Elks with Johnnie Bean
Cool ass brother was always on the scene

Good, Wonderful, Fond memories but there is some sadness
Red and Blue Violence it created some Madness
Pomona's no joke and I know you know
It can be a Cold Place without no snow
Cause we lost some good friends along the way,
That's why I want to take this time to say
If by violence, accident, an illness, untimely release
I shout out love, respect and wish you peace
Being from Pomona you had to be a beast.

My Mama. Ms. Stewart worked at Pomona City Jail
Came home everyday, never did she fail
To say "Loni and Kim do all your friends go to jail?
We answer dang mama "who'd you put in cell?

She's say your friends was at Zody's and they got caught stealing
Your homeboy too he got caught dealing
Mixed emotions and real strong feelings

My next line I'm a say twice cause I want to repeat
Insane, Chalie Mac, BoBo, MC, Mark and Tweet,
If you don't know them names, then you didn't know them streets

Kutzee, Lil Rat, Fatt Matt and Troy (aka) Frog
Hanging on Belinda man I miss my dog
 Lady, Linda, Lenny, Clarisse, and Denise
Trips me out all five **Died** but **Lived** on my street

Jackie, Darlene, Finette, Kathy and Milfaye
All are still loved and missed to this day

Len Dog, Machine GunWillie and Sugar Hill Neal
Don't ya'll remember William aka Mr. Bill
My friend, Tyrone Blanche and cool Ass Nate
I cried as each one left for the Pearlie gate

I was on the phone reading this poem to the home girl Dee Big
She said, Damn girl you so talented, that's real good, I dig!
"But you left out Tony Godfather and of course Big Flan"
I said "oh your baby daddy, Asshole Flan was your man"

Tony Godfather did come to my house looking for Killer Kool
to shoot dice
I would be pissed off, but I'd say "Bust his ass twice"
I gambled under the street light with Dirt and Donnie my friends,
Running to my house every time I lost my ends,
I would snatch up my money in the blink of an eye
Quick, fast and in a hurry no time to say bye
They would chase me home and to my house I would run
All the while screaming
" **YOU KNOW WE WAS JUST PLAYING FOR FUN"**

On my street " Arthur Ave" lived Bandit, G. Ron, Dirt, Donnie, and cool ass Alvin Lee,
The only one in Pomona that I know stroll colder than me,
well maybe , Let me think cause, there was that FEE FEE

Crazy Larry, Dwayne Damper, Baby Boy, Cabbage, Fub and Huck
Some banging, Hustling, gambling and chasing that buck
 Jeff , Kenny, Rodeo Joe, The Jenkins brothers, Walter and Mel
The Maxwells, the Johns, the Randalls, the Bells

Can't forget my OG'S from the other side of P town
You know how they got down… and NO… they didn't mess around

Lovejoy, Valhalla, Vassar, Lennox and Hallwood
Hanging on the block you knew where you stood
From the Rue was crew that most everybody knew
There Was Kasha, Carmella, the warden and Shonie Poo

D'juan, Tim Charles, Baby Lloyd, and Big Rick
Can't forget the homie known as Tom Slick
The General and his brothers Tracy and Jeff
Soldier's right there didn't take no mess

Lil Hayward, Lil Larry, Lil Lloyd aka Chu Chu
You can't even imagine how much we all love and miss you!

Wow!   Man!   That's just too much grief
Life is too short   Let us end all beef
My friends sleep easy…… please rest in Peace
My prayer to God is that pain all cease

To all of us that remain and have been left behind,
Mend our hearts totally and please be kind
There is only this one chance…. there is no rewind

Praying consistently to stay in our right mind

And this may have been a long poem to endure
But I'm a spit this Love while I'm right here on this floor

Shout out to Pomona and all of you that I truly love
Here on this earth today and those ABOVE
I'm going to end it soon although I could say more
I didn't forget Indian Hill Swap meet or the fish store.

If I didn't hit you in this poem, PLEASE don't feel overlooked
Chances are that you made the book
A chapter, a verse or a line in this poem
Just a lot of love because Pomona's my home

You see,   you see... you see......you see.
I was a little girl that moved from Pittsburgh PA to the heart of Pomona CA.
Steady ready... sometimes petty, but I like things my way, same friends since back in the day
Never banged! not one day, Own my own business...
but I still love to play
Still talking shit, still having my say
My city my way.... straight from Pomona CA
For life and then some

46

WORD PLAY

Some people, like to sit on the couch...Play games... and smoke Herbs
As for me, I just like to play with Words

I play with words **LIKE** how some people play with relationships and money
Like how your friend tell a joke that ain't even funny

 NOW, Emily did you catch that simile? I know you have the Ability Mind sharp.... Agility... stability....... far from senility.
That's why you're here and not in that facility
                Right?
It's No fun .... when it's no pun intended,
Find a broken verb I will mend it
Predicate or adjective   a sentence independent
You can borrow money but only because I lend it

I'll spin it around and send it back from sad to funny.
I'll make a bee sick from eating its own honey
It may be Dark outside but I'll make it sunny
But Only after you paid me my money

Word choice, the volume of the voice,
Right tone when you're in the zone
Euphemisms, spoonerisms and ambiguous
Linked it together and make it continuous

My Tongue twister
Is designed to make your mind blister
Cut up, bandaged In need of peroxide
That analogy should make you hide
Too ambiguous? Let me call you a ride
That's a Double meaning with two sides

This syntax should help you   relax
Throw up the ball and pick up the jax
Skate through life like you're on floor wax
Too many words!   Have I exceeded my max?

A metaphor should leave you on the floor,
With your hand over one eye wanting more
Shivering, shaking, crawling for the door
That's the job of a hard core metaphor

Literally or figuratively
Genuinely .... I can't stand bigotry
BUT
I love me some words.......... PLEASE let them live
Fresh new meaning   to them we give
Words convey the things we need to say
Communicating a big part of each day
Scramble it....mix it.... twist it.... say it your way
Then Shout **Abra cadabra!** cause you made words play

47

HOT FLASH

When my friend would have a hot flash,
I would usually just laugh at her ass,

 now the jOKES on me as the sweat drips to my knee,
Live long enough and you too will see
This is no joke believe you me

heat rising from my feet all the way to my head,
sheets full of sweat that ruins my bed,

It feels like someone actually set you on fire
A wish for relief is your only desire.

She described the feeling as her own personal summer,
getting old and menopause is such a bummer,

belly fat, bad knees and achy joints
I CAN'T understand what is the point

midlife crisis Is WHAT'S next?
It's hard to put this all in to context

hormonal imbalances and wanting to cry
changes in my body I can not deny

menopause is real is scary
will I get real hairy?

ON my face, Please Lord not my chin
how long does it last? when does it end

Quickly it came out of the blue
Good thing it lasts only a minute to two
That's the reason, why I keep a fan in my purse
For some Air, to minimize this curse

Hot flash hot flash Here Comes one now
Someone be kind and pass me a towel

Out of the blue, quickly it came
Real talk, no joke, menopause is no game

48

LACTOSE INTOLERANT

What the hell, but time will tell, when you about forty-one
Partied out, tired, restless, damn near done
Then, you find out some new shit, not nearly fun
I thought wasn't nothing new under this sun

You see, I started to notice something at thirty nine
It was always after I had dined
On some enchiladas or some mac n cheese
It came upon me like a stone cold breeze

You see...........

I used to drink milk, eat cheese and lick a cone
Now my tummy hurt and I need time alone
Time to release the big cyclone

Rumble tumble and full of gas
Even Vanilla bean, can't pass
How long this shit supposed to last

Dang! what happened to my ass.
To the toilet, to the toilet, to the toilet...I run ever so quickly
When the fuck I start getting so sickly
Can't pull down my pant quick enough
Need to hurry before I splatter this stuff

In the stall, on the toilet thinking
Meditating, reading and stinking,
Saying damn, what is it that I ate?
Not sure bit it tasted great.

I love you food, but you don't like me
Now all of sudden we don't agree
 SO.......
I'm lactose intolerant and that's a fact
No more dairy.....totally whack
Beano, gas relief I got it packed
I keeps it handy in the knapsack

Nightmare wishes and caviar dreams
I still won't be denied my ice cream

49

WHY WOULD YOU WEAR YOUR PAJAMAS TO THE DMV?

Why would you wear your pajamas the DMV?
Why would you do that to your community?
you want everyone to know you don't give a damn
and you don't pay taxes to Uncle Sam

You wear Betty Boop and he wears Sponge Bob
well, together you look like two slobs
Nere one of you bums can't keep job

It only take a minute to put on some shorts
but you will probably wear them to court
and tell the judge that your sorry
it's too too late cuz he seen you on Maury

In your life, don't you want more?
Then why would you wear them to the store?

your pants are right there on the floor
by your old beer, blunt and dirty draws
Now you mad and want to throw them paws

Cause people look at you like your scum
wondering where you're from
the projects, the ghetto, the barrio, the street
around the corner from the swap meet

People see you and avoid eye contact
cause no one wants to watch they back
This is just my opinion and not a fact

but I think

you're lazy, shiftless and have no ambition
I wonder if you are afraid of life and competition
In the world, you gotta get dressed to get ahead
you can't just roll out the bed

Brush your teeth and wash your face
get it together and get in the race

get up, get dressed and have a good day
I know you got some shit to say
make it happen, have it your way
but please, please, don't wear your pajamas to the DMV
or your slippers either

50

HEAVENLY BOUND BUT NO EARTHLY GOOD

You say you're sanctified and filled with the Holy Ghost
But you the one gossiping the most
Never Humble and quick to boast
Wouldn't offer the homeless a piece of toast

Walk by folks with your nose all in the air
People don't speak because they fear
Your judgment, wrath and your unfriendly smile
You been wearing that frown for a while now

Holier than thou and full of grace
Can't count the number of folks you chased
Out the church and into the world
With your self-righteous lip curled

Never a good morning and will barely speak
Missed many chances to minister to the weak

It's only love and kindness they seek
But your nose was high as mountain peak

You're so heavenly bound but no earthly good
Never done nothing in your neighborhood
You often reply, "If I could I would"
Then claim to be too busy and misunderstood

Nope it's clear you just playing a role
You wear some parts of the armor but not the whole
Breastplate of righteousness (Check) yeah you got that
It goes good with that new church hat

Your sword, you keeps that in a nice leather case
Right beside your mirror to see your two face

Gird up your loins with the truth
But make sure that you're beyond reproof
Did you correctly divide the word of truth?

Oh Church……If I could only get you to see
That the helmet of salvation is still free

It was paid with a heavy price
I think you could be a little than just a little nice

To those who are different, and not where you're at, or that have a need
For your love they shouldn't have to plead
Isn't it the place of the church to lead?

With the gospel feet of peace into his heart
Time to stop this nonsense and do your part
Loving your neighbor is not a lost art

Confession of sin is a good place to start

To whom much is given, much is required and that
is your reasonable service
Don't be so heavenly bound that you are no earthly good

51

THE RETURN OF THE SPARKLE

by Beverly Ann Braxton (AKA) Afi (My Maternal Aunt)

You seem to know the magic that I need
You seem to put the Sparkle
Back in me
The smiles have returned
My heart ekes warmth again
Since you put the Sparkle
Back in me
When I first met you
I couldn't believe my eyes
You swept me off my feet
Taking me by surprise
You seem to put the Sparkle
Back in me
The Warmth we Shared
As you kissed away my tears
Just seemed to put the Sparkle
Back in me

52

MEMORY LANE

by Marla Stewart (My Mother)

I'm taking a trip down memory lane.
My mind's the conductor; jump on my train.
I'll show you things you wouldn't believe.
They'll make you laugh. They'll make you grieve.
Maybe you'll cry, but that's ok.
Step in my mind, we're on the way.
Going back a few years, take a look and see.
No, never mind, too much misery.
Let's go a little bit further back
And see what we can to the right of the track.
It's getting clear. It's a person. A friend?
No, that's just a tree blowing in the wind.
What do we have here on the other side?
Oh yeah, that's the time I became a bride?
I got married to......*Oh,*..... What's his name?
It doesn't matter. I lost that game.
There seems to be something blocking the way.
What is it?   Why the delay?
I'm sorry. Trip's over.   My Mind can't recall.
Right on the track, I have built a brick wall.

Kim Braxton
(AKA)
Kacee Kemiah
**KACEE MEANS GREAT, KEMIAH MEANS QUEEN
STRAIGHT FROM THE MOTHERLAND RED, BLACK AND GREEN
BY WAY OF PITTSBURGH PA AND POMONA CA.**

Kim Braxton (AKA) Kacee Kemiah is an American poet and Spoken Word Artist. As an empowered African-American woman, she seeks to share her life experiences with others with the aim of fostering understanding and tolerance. Her poems and book reflect insights gained through her life experiences which include social activism, female empowerment and relationships. Kim has been a Licensed Clinical Social Worker for over 20 years in a Forensic Hospital and as a Psychotherapist in Group Homes in the Community. She is as entertaining as she is insightful, which makes her poetry and book real Edgy, Engaging and Thought Provoking. Kacee has performed and perfected her craft throughout the Inland Empire.

www.ingramcontent.com/pod-product-compliance
Lightning Source LLC
LaVergne TN
LVHW051950060526
838201LV00059B/3591